JUST REWARDS

or
Who Is That Man in the Moon
&
What's He Doing Up There Anyway?

by **Steve Sanfield** • *illustrated by* **Emily Lisker**

Orchard Books • *New York*

Orchard Books, 95 Madison Avenue, New York, NY 10016

Manufactured in the United States of America. Printed by Barton Press,
Inc. Bound by Horowitz/Rae. Book design by Jean Krulis. The text of this
book is set in 14 point Perpetua Bold. The illustrations are oil on canvas
reproduced in full color.

10 9 8 7 6 5 4 3 2 1

Library of Congress Cataloging-in-Publication Data. Sanfield, Steve. Just rewards, or, Who is that man in the moon & what's he
doing up there anyway? / by Steve Sanfield ; illustrated by Emily Lisker.   p. cm. "A Richard Jackson book"—Half t.p. Summary:
An original interpretation of a Chinese folktale which explains the presence of the man in the moon.   ISBN 0-531-09535-5. —
ISBN 0-531-08885-5 (lib. bdg.)   [1. Folklore—China.]   I. Lisker, Emily, ill.   II. Title. PZ8.1.S242Ju   1996   398.2'0951—dc20
[E]   95-51563

A NOTE ON THE STORY

From the very beginning we humans have been trying to explain the world around us
through stories. There seems to be no culture that does not have its tale about the markings
we see on the moon. To the Yakuts of Siberia it's a young girl with her water buckets. To the
Jibaro of Ecuador it's a man trying to escape his nagging wife. And among different tribes of
North American Indians it could be an owl, a rabbit, or three frog sisters.

Throughout much of Asia (China, Japan, Korea, Vietnam) the "man in the moon" is
often portrayed as a greedy person who is being punished for some evil deed he's done in his
blind pursuit of wealth. This particular version, though based on stories found in Wolfram
Eberhard's *Folktales of China* and Louise and Yuan Hsi Kuo's *Chinese Folktales*, is my own interpretation that developed through many years of telling it to American schoolchildren.

To Sarah—S.S.

To Bill—E.L.

Not so long ago, and not so far away, there lived two farmers who were friends and neighbors. They were very different kinds of men. One was kind and gentle, as most of you are. The other was stingy and greedy and mean. But because they were neighbors, they were wise enough to remain friends.

One bright spring morning they were strolling along the path by the riverbank, and there under an ancient willow they found a tiny sparrow with a broken wing.

The kind, gentle man bent down and picked it up. "Oh, you poor bird," he said tenderly. "You've got a broken wing."

"What are you wasting your time with that for?" mockcd his neighbor.

"This bird's hurt. I'm going to take it home and try to heal it."

"Oh, you've always been such a fool," laughed the stingy, greedy man.

The kind, gentle man did not listen. He took that bird home, and each day he brought it water and worms and insects. And each day the bird became stronger and stronger until its wing was completely healed.

Then he carried the bird to his garden, held it in the palm of his hand, and said, "Little bird, your wing is healed now. You can fly away home."

And that bird turned to that man, opened its beak, and spoke to him (spoke to him just as I'm speaking to you now). "Because of what you have done for me, because of your kindness, I want you to have your just reward."

The tiny sparrow dropped a tiny seed into the farmer's palm. "Plant this in your garden, and you will have your just reward."

With that, the bird flew away into the blue sky.

The kind, gentle man planted the seed. All spring and summer he hoed it and weeded it and watered it, and out of that tiny seed grew a magnificent watermelon vine.

The vine snaked and
twisted all through his garden, and it was
hung with round, plump, luscious-looking watermelons.

When the harvest moon was full and bright, the farmer began to pick his crop. He picked the first melon and *POP!* Out poured shiny silver coins.

He picked the next one and *POP!* Out poured glistening gold coins.

He picked the next one and *POP!* Out poured precious polished pearls.

Each time he picked a melon, *POP! POP! POP!* Diamonds. Emeralds. Rubies. More riches than he had ever dreamed of or imagined. He was now a wealthy man—one of the wealthiest men in the entire land.

Naturally the kind, gentle man wanted to share the news of his good fortune with his neighbor.

"Oh, that's wonderful," mumbled the stingy, greedy man when he heard. "I'm very happy for you," he said through a tight, tight smile.

But we know, don't we, that's not what he really felt. No. He was overcome with envy and resentment and desire.

Why shouldn't I be rich? he thought to himself. *Why shouldn't I have my own reward? I know what I'll do. I'll find a bird with a broken wing. I'll heal it, and then I'll get my reward.*

The stingy, greedy man ran to the path by the river. He walked up and down, up and down, looking for a bird with a broken wing, but he did not find one. He returned the next day and walked up and down, up and down, but still he could not find one.

Finally on the third day he lost all his patience. He reached into his pocket and pulled out a slingshot. *WHAP!* He shot a sparrow right out of the willow tree.

He kneeled down and picked it up roughly. "Aw, you poor, poor bird," he said almost as if he cared. "How terrible. You've got a broken wing. But I'll tell you what I'll do. I'll help you to heal it."

"You just be sure I get my reward."

That stingy, greedy man did just as he said. He took the
injured bird home. And each day he brought it water and worms

and insects, and each day he would remind the sparrow, "Don't forget what I'm doing for you, and don't you forget my reward."

When the bird's wing had healed, the farmer carried it to his garden, held it firmly, and said, "So, bird, you're all fixed up now. You can go. But before you do, you'd better give me my reward."

That bird turned to that man, opened its beak, and spoke to him (spoke to him just as I'm speaking to you now). "Yes. Because of what you've done, because of the way you've treated me, I want you to have your just reward."

The sparrow dropped a tiny seed into the stingy, greedy man's palm and told him, "Plant this in your garden, and you, too, will have your just reward." Then, as quickly as it could, the bird flew off.

The stingy, greedy man ran to his garden and planted the seed. All spring and summer he hoed it and weeded it and watered it, working harder than he had ever worked in his life, and out of that tiny seed grew another magnificent watermelon vine.

However, this vine did not snake and twist through his garden. No. It grew straight up out of the ground and then began to wind its way into the sky. And the strangest thing of all was that not a single melon could be seen anywhere.

What does this mean? he wondered. *Where are my watermelons? Where's my reward?*

All summer long the vine grew higher and higher and higher until finally, on the night of the full harvest moon, it had grown so high it reached the face of the cold, lonely moon itself.

When the stingy, greedy man saw that, he whooped, "Ahaa! I
understand. I understand. All the riches of the moon for me. All
for me. Ha, ha, ha!" He pounded his chest. He jumped for joy.
He shouted and laughed. "Ha, ha, ha! All the riches of the moon
are mine, all mine. Mine. Mine. Mine. I'm rich. Rich. Rich. Rich.
Even richer than my foolish neighbor."

Then he leaped onto the vine. He climbed and he climbed and he climbed and he climbed, all the time dreaming of the wealth that would soon be his. *Jewels. Gold. Silver. All mine. Mine. Mine. Mine.*

He climbed and he climbed and he climbed some more until at last he reached the cold, lonely moon. With a single giant step he was upon it, and at that instant the vine withered and died. He had absolutely no way to get off the moon.

If, on a clear night, you go outside and look hard enough, you just might be able to see that stingy, greedy man in the moon, because . . . he's still there.